GW01459088

The
A-Z
OF BEING
IRISH

This edition first published 2025 by
The O'Brien Press Ltd,
12 Terenure Road East, Rathgar,
Dublin 6, D06 HD27, Ireland.
Tel: +353 1 4923333; Fax: +353 1 4922777
E-mail: books@obrien.ie; website: obrien.ie.
First published in hardback 2018.
The O'Brien Press is a member of Publishing Ireland.

ISBN: 978-1-78849-564-6

Text © copyright Sarah Cassidy & Kunak McGann 2018
The moral rights of the authors have been asserted.
Copyright for typesetting, layout, editing, design © The O'Brien Press Ltd
Cover and internal design by Emma Byrne.

All rights reserved.

No part of this publication may be reproduced or utilised in any form or by
any means, electronic or mechanical, including for text and data mining,
training artificial intelligence systems, photocopying, recording or in any information
storage and retrieval system, without permission in writing from the publisher.

1 3 5 7 8 6 4 2
25 26 27 28 29

Printed and bound by and bound by Drukarnia Skleniarz, Poland.
The paper in this book is produced using pulp from managed forests.

Published in
DUBLIN
UNESCO
City of Literature

Great Irish books
O'BRIEN
obrien.ie

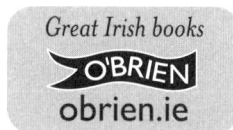

The
A-Z
OF BEING
IRISH

Sarah Cassidy & Kunak McGann

THE O'BRIEN PRESS
DUBLIN

A

AA Roadwatch

/ey ey rohd-woch/

proper noun. commuter intelligence

The ultimate source of random Irish place names. Where else could you hear of exotic locations like the Lough Atalia Road, the Moneenageisha junction and the townland of Blackhall Big, as well as the Dunkettle Interchange, stop-go systems and a jam-packed M50? For many years, it was our breakfast-time obsession.

accent

/ak-sent/

noun. seductive speech pattern

Regularly voted the sexiest in the world, beating out the Scottish, Italian and French, our accent may be the best thing we Irish have going for us. And we're not afraid to use it. Of course, some Irish accents are easier to understand than others, but from the lyrical Donegal lilt to the strong Cork brogue, foreigners find we all have one thing in common: 'turty-tree and a turd.'

Amhrán na bhFiann

/ow-rawn na vee-un/

song. Ireland's national anthem

Translating as 'The Soldier's Song', this patriotic tune was written back in the early 1900s but wasn't officially adopted as our national anthem until 1926. Featuring some tricky Irish words, nowadays it is mimed and mumbled by school kids all over the country – especially that last line: '*Shoving Connie around the fiiiiiiiiiiiiiiiiiiiiiiiiiiiiiield!*'

Angelus

/an-juh-lus/

proper noun. tolling of the bell for prayer

Bong – Bong – Bong. The national broadcaster's longest-running and most-watched religious programme, the Angelus still rings out on RTÉ One at six o'clock every evening, and on Radio 1 at noon and 6pm. Traditionally a call to prayer, for a lot of Irish families it was simply a short pause between mouthfuls of dinner.

Aran jumper

/ar-in jump-ur/

proper noun. snazzy Irish knitwear

Legend has it that each Aran Island fisherman wore a
jumper knitted with a distinct family pattern so that, if
lost at sea, he would be easily identifiable by the stitching
on his Aran jumper. A great story but, alas, probably not
true. For most Irish kids, your tight-fitting Aran jumper
was usually knitted by your least favourite aunt and was
UNBELIEVABLY scratchy.

B

B*Witched

/bee-wich-d/

proper noun. double-denim-clad girl band

This Irish-dancing foursome hit the charts in the late-1990s and had teenagers doing their 1, 2, 3's up and down the dance floors. And they fought like their Da as well.

bacon & cabbage

/bey-kun und kab-ij/

noun. delicious culinary pairing

Nutritionally balanced for a great midweek family dinner, bacon & cabbage goes head-to-head with Irish stew for the title of Ireland's national dish. And just the idea of this combo sets mouths watering all over the country. Mmmmmm … boiled meat.

Baileys

/bey-leez/

proper noun. the original Irish cream

First produced in 1974, Baileys is made with whiskey, cream and a number of top-secret ingredients. Granted, it has a bit of a reputation for appealing to an older demographic, and it's definitely Great-Aunt Maura's favourite drink, but we're all guilty of the odd sweet-toothed nightcap. And sure it just wouldn't be the festive season without a bit of Baileys. Handy tip: try a little on your cornflakes on Christmas morning.

B&Bs

/bee und beez/

noun pl. rented resting place

Homes away from home for tourists looking for an authentic Irish experience and wedding guests who refuse to pay extortionate hotel prices. In the past, B&Bs were renowned for framed pictures of the Sacred Heart hanging above lumpy beds. But with all the notions these days, don't be surprised if you get a bit of avocado with your toast in the morning. Fancy!

banshee

/ban-shee/

noun. ominous female spirit

The shriek of the wild-haired banshee is said to signal
an impending death, particularly for five Irish families:
the O'Briens, O'Neills, O'Connors, Kavanaghs and
O'Gradys. Banshees have even been known to follow Irish
people abroad, screeching outside soon-to-be-bereaved
emigrants' houses. She is literally the stalker from hell.

Barack Obama Plaza

/bar-ak oh-ba-ma pla-za/

proper noun. a service station fit for a president

The former U.S. President can trace his roots back
to Moneygall in County Offaly and in 2011 was
enthusiastically welcomed 'home'. If he ever returns he can
drop by the M7 petrol station named in his honour and
pick up a 'What's the craic, Barack?' t-shirt, a 'My name is
Barack Obama of the Moneygall O'Bamas and I've come
home to find the apostrophe we lost along the way'
badge, or even a stick of Obama Plaza rock.

barmbrack

/barm-brak/

noun. fortune-telling fruit loaf

An Irish fruit cake loaded with sultanas and dried peel, barmbrack is delicious spread with butter and served with a cup of tea. Traditionally eaten around Halloween, when it often contains a hidden ring or coins that are thought to bring good luck to whoever is fortunate enough not to choke on them.

Barry's Tea ad

/bar-eez tee ad/

proper noun. trip down memory lane

You know it's that time of year when you hear the Barry's Tea train-set ad. Played on Irish radio every Christmas since 1994 and voiced by the late Peter Caffrey, this nostalgic ad always brings a warm glow. 'Santa will bring them what they want, I said. This one's from me. Put the kettle on and we'll have a cup of tea.'

battle of the brands

/ba-tul uv thuh branz/

phrase. lifelong allegiances

When we Irish pick a side, we're fierce loyal. You're either Lyons or you're Barry's. You're Tayto or you're King. You're Guinness or you're Murphy's. And don't you dare bring a Chef bottle into a Heinz house (even if it's 50% off).

begrudgery

/bi-gruj-ur-ee/

noun. homegrown resentment of success

The Irish? A nation of begrudgers? I wouldn't have thought so. Sure aren't we fierce proud of Saoirse Ronan and Chris O'Dowd and U2? Well, maybe not U2. Bloody Bono and his mansion in Dalkey and his sunglasses. He wears them indoors, you know. *Indoors?!* Who does he think he is?

Bestie

/jorj best/

person. Belfast footballing hero

'If I had to choose between dribbling past five players and scoring from forty yards at Anfield or shagging Miss World, it'd be a hard choice. Thankfully, I've done both.'
George Best, top scorer, in his own words.

Big Fella

/big fel-a/

person. Cork-born rebel and heartthrob

Michael Collins was only 31 when he was shot dead at Béal na Bláth, Co. Cork, in 1922. Every Valentine's Day his grave at Glasnevin Cemetery is covered with flowers and cards from women all over the world sending their love to the 'Big Fella'. Could have *something* to do with the hugely successful Hollywood biopic and a handsome Liam Neeson parading around Dublin in uniform.

Big Snow of '82

/big snoh uv ey-tee-too/

event. historically cold winter

The winter that went down in Irish legend as the worst
in living memory, when the whole country ground to a
halt and Irish children finally got to make some decent
snowmen. With widespread electricity cuts, 100,000
homes and businesses lost power. There were actual
bread riots, and the government had to requisition 50,000
gallons of milk to combat the dairy drought in the capital.
We thought it was the worst we'd see. And then came
the Big Snow of 2018 …

blaa

/blaaaa/

noun. celebrated Waterford bread roll

Forget the paleo diet, the Irish have long had a love affair
with bread – from slabs of homemade soda bread topped
with smoked salmon to warm toast slathered in real
butter. King of the breads has got to be the Waterford
blaa, a soft or crusty white roll with a sweet, malty flavour.
Dear Lord, give us our daily bread.

black pudding

/blak pud-ing/

noun. blood sausage

Made from pig's blood (and a great source of protein
and iron), for years black pudding played second fiddle
to white pudding as part of an Irish fry-up. Now it's
sought after by top chefs and foodies and served as an
accompaniment to succulent scallops or perfectly poached
eggs. It may have developed notions . . .

blessing of the graves

/bles-ing uv thuh greyvz/

event. Catholic ritual

Just when you think you have the weekend to yourself,
Mammy reminds you that the blessing of the graves is on
Sunday. Cue standing around your grandad's grave for a
couple of hours and nodding at people you haven't seen
since this time last year, as Fr. O'Connor makes his way
around the graveyard with his megaphone and an extra
pep in his step. Blessing of the graves aficionados never
forget their foldaway stool, umbrella, sun cream and a few
snacks. This could be a long one.

blessings

/bles-ingz/

noun pl. wishes for good fortune

May the road rise to meet you. May you always be blessed with walls for the wind. May the roof above us never fall in, and may the friends gathered below it never fall out. Who cares what they mean? They sound authentic and look good on a fridge magnet.

Bloomsday

/bloomz-dey/

event. James Joyce celebration

If you spot a bunch of people wearing straw boaters and Edwardian garb, you haven't lost your mind – it's Bloomsday. Named for Leopold Bloom, the central character in James Joyce's *Ulysses*, and celebrated each year on 16th June, Bloomsday involves costumed people swanning around Dublin taking in locations visited by Mr. Bloom and quoting their favourite passages. Chances are most of them never finished the tome … or even started it.

blow-ins

/bloh-inz/

person pl. outsiders

Anyone who wasn't born and bred in the area or can't trace their local lineage back at least three generations. Once a blow-in, always a blow-in.

BOD

/bry-un oh dris-kul/

person. rugby giant

One of the most capped players in rugby union history. Leading Six Nations try scorer. Ireland's leading try scorer. Captained Ireland to its first Grand Slam in sixty-one years. Is Brian O'Driscoll the greatest rugby player of all time? Quite possibly. And look who his missus is. In BOD we trust.

bodhrán

/bow-rawn/

noun. Irish percussion

A traditional Irish drum that evolved from the tambourine.
Even talentless beginners can make a stab at playing it. If
you ever find yourself at a sing-song but haven't a note in
your head, grab a bodhrán and give it an auld bang during
the chorus. Up, ya boyo!

Bosco

/boss-koh/

person. cult puppet

A much-loved red-haired puppet who lived in a box
and entertained Irish kids throughout the 1980s. Well,
entertained might be a stretch – how many times can
you go to the zoo or the Cadbury's factory through the
Magic Door? And let's not forget all of Bosco's buddies,
both human and plasticine, who made that TV licence fee
worthwhile.

boy bands

/boi banz/

noun pl. manufactured male pop

The Carter Twins, Jedward, D-Side and OTT: Ireland has produced its fair share of quality boy bands. Boyzone were the first to hit the big time, paving the way for Westlife, who matched the record of the Beatles by having seven consecutive number ones. When it came to sitting on a stool and rising triumphantly for the key change, the Irish had the rest of the world beat.

Braveheart

/breyv-hart/

film. full-throated Scottish epic

Much of it filmed in the historic town of Trim in the Royal County, *Braveheart* brought Hollywood to Ireland. Rumours abounded about where the cast was sleeping, drinking and eating. Half the residents of Meath claimed to have had the bants with Willam Wallace in the flesh. All together now: 'They may take our lives, but they will never take our freedom!'

breakfast roll

/brek-fast rohl/

noun. baguette with copious filling

Ever popular with taxi drivers and construction workers, this fry-up in a roll will definitely keep you going till lunchtime. Sausages, bacon, white pudding, black pudding, mushrooms, tomatoes, egg, ketchup or brown sauce. Keep it coming!

brown sauce

/brown saws/

noun. russet condiment

Takes half an hour to get it out of the bottle, but for brown sauce devotees it's worth it – sure it goes with spuds, bread, meat, cheese, anything you fancy. Ireland's Marmite equivalent: you love it or you hate it.

bye bye bye bye bye

/by by by by by/

phrase. repeated farewell

Why do Irish people find it so hard to finish a phone call?

C

carvery

/kar-vur-ee/

noun. communal roast

If you like four varieties of spud for your dinner, then carvery is the meal for you. Served in pubs and hotels throughout the country, this staple of the Irish diet provides all the sustenance you could possibly need. Thick slices of ham and turkey or roast beef served with any amount of veg and a *lot* of potato (think mash, roast, croquettes, chips) all drenched in gravy. Usually comes with a complimentary glass of dilutable orange to wash it all down. Wear your stretchy trousers.

Catholicism

/kath-ol-uh-siz-m/

proper noun. Christian religion of the Roman variety

Despite falling numbers, Catholicism is still the leading religion in Ireland – by a country mile. Nowadays there is a sliding scale of Catholics that goes something like this: devout, à la carte, lapsed, and returning because you need to get your child into the local school (cue scores of beefy five-year-olds running up the aisle to get baptised before enrolment day).

Celtic Tiger

/kel-tik ty-gur/

phrase. booming Irish economy

Weekend trips to NYC to stock up on your Tommy 'Highflier' and your Ralph 'La'wren', holiday homes in Bulgaria, and more credit-card debt than you can shake a platinum-ringed finger at? For some, the Celtic Tiger roared – for others, it merely miaowed quietly in the corner.

The Chat

/thuh chat/

noun. a bit of banter

Irish people will talk to ANYONE. Just ask that lad sitting on his own at the bar trying to have a quiet pint.

Cheltenham

/chelt-un-um/

event. annual horse racing festival

Week booked off work? Check!
Overdraft secured? Check!
Top Tips obtained from yer man who knows the jockey
who's a friend of yer man riding one of the horses? Check!

A week of horse racing when the Irish take on the British,
and people who don't know their soft ground from their
hard throw away their hard-earned cash on the hopes of
winning big.

Child of Prague

/chyld uv praag/

person. religious statuette

A wooden statue of a young Jesus from the 16th century
and located in – you've guessed it – Prague. Copies
became popular in Catholic countries all over the world,
and Ireland was no exception. Here, the little Czech
guy is thought to have special powers over the weather.
Getting married? Place this miraculous statue in your
garden overnight and the rain is guaranteed to move
elsewhere for your big day.

chipper

/chip-ur/

noun. fast food establishment

The chipper is an institution here – run by those famous Irish dynasties, the Borzas, the Macaris, the Romas and the Genoas. Home to the overflowing snack box and the entire-day's-calories-worth chicken kebab, the enigmatic spice burger and the dubious battered sausage, there's no better place to be at 2am. And the vinegar at home NEVER tastes the same.

Cidona

/sy-dohn-a/

proper noun. fruity fizziness

A sparkling apple-based soft drink reminiscent of cider and madly popular in Ireland in the 1980s. Give one to the child and sure they can pretend they're having a 'grown-up' drink too.

ciotóg

/kit-ohg/

person. awkward writer

The Irish word for a left-hander, ciotóg also means 'strange one' and there used to be vicious rumours that left-handers had been touched by the Devil himself. Definitely not to be trusted.

Claddagh ring

/kla-da ring/

proper noun. traditional Irish bling

Famously worn by celebs like Jim Morrison, Walt Disney and Liam Gallagher, the Claddagh is a traditional Irish ring depicting a crown-wearing heart clasped between two hands. If you're in love, wear the ring with the heart pointing inwards, towards your heart, and if you are looking for love, point it out. An Irish forerunner of the Facebook relationship status.

coddle

/kod-ul/

noun. not altogether enticing meat dish

Synonymous with our capital city, this dish consists of boiled sausages, bacon and potato in stock. It looks about as appetising as it sounds, but there sure is eating and drinking in it. Close your eyes and think of Dublin.

The Commitments

/thuh kom-it-muntz/

film. best Irish flick ever

Who didn't want to grab their best buds, dust off their tin whistle (I'm sure we can make this sound just like a saxophone . . .) and form their own band after seeing *The Commitments* for the first time? Based on Roddy Doyle's best-selling novel, it brought us Joey 'The Lips' Fagan, Jimmy 'The Bollix' Rabbitte and the soulful voices of Imelda, Natalie, Bernie and Deco. Best film soundtrack. Bar none.

Community Games

/kom-yoon-it-ee geymz/

event. fierce national children's competition

Qualifying for the Community Games is like reaching the Irish Kid Olympics. The very act of making it to the Games means you have seen off local competition and are ready to compete at national level. The country's top young athletes, GAA players and artists (yes, artists, it's not all about sport, you know) converge to compete against their rivals and gain bragging rights for life.

confession

/kon-fesh-un/

noun. disclosure of sins

If you attended Catholic school in Ireland, chances are you have uttered the words 'Bless me Father for I have sinned. It has been [insert acceptable amount of time here] since my last confession. These are my sins . . .' normally followed by a banal list of your failings as a child: fighting with family, swearing, etc. The best part was comparing penances with your classmates after and wondering, just what did Máire get up to to earn herself five Hail Marys and ten Our Fathers?

Confirmation

/kon-fur-mey-shun/

event. Catholic coming-of-age

The final religious ceremony bestowed on young Irish Catholics before they leave primary school and daily religious instruction behind. Also when they take THE PLEDGE – a commitment not to touch a drop of alcohol until they turn eighteen. Good luck with that …

contraception

/kon-tra-sep-shun/

noun. to be sure to be sure

Ireland was notoriously late to the party when it came to contraception. It was only in 1985 when Frankie Goes to Hollywood welcomed us to the Pleasuredome and Madonna urged us to get into the groove that Ireland finally legalised condoms without prescription. Before then it was an emotionally scarring lecture about honourable intentions from the family doctor.

Copper Face Jacks

/kop-ur feys jaks/

place name. cultural phenomenon

Probably the best-known nightclub in Ireland, Coppers
is open and heaving every night of the week. There are
guards, teachers and nurses literally hanging off the walls. If
ya can't pull in Coppers, there's no hope for ya.

country music

/kun-tree myoo-zik/

noun. yee haw!

In Nashville they sing about losing their wives, their dogs,
their Cadillacs and their homes. In Ireland we prefer
to celebrate childhood biscuits. Anyone for a Wagon
Wheel?

county colours

/kown-tee kul-urz/

noun pl. shades of allegiance

Your Daddy's from Cork. Your Mammy's from Galway.
You live in Kildare. You can mix and match your jerseys
when there's nothing at stake, but when one team is
pitched against another, what do you do? What in God's
name do you do??

cows

/kowz/

noun pl. domesticated bovines

At around seven million, cows now clock in at a much
higher population than people in Ireland. But we don't
just keep them around for their milk and their meat. For
people in the know, cows are great at predicting the
weather – if they're lying down, stick your raincoat on or
grab a brolly; if they're standing up, slather on the factor 50.
Udderly foolproof.

COYBIG

/kum awn yoo boyz in green/

phrase. cheering on the Irish team

Everyone's favourite Facebook status the day before the Big Match. The day after, prepare for something a little less upbeat when the realities of being an Irish fan hit home.

craic

/krak/

noun. enjoyment

'What's the craic?' 'Isn't yer man some craic?' 'Ah, we had some craic last night.' 'The craic was mighty.' No, not the illegal drug but the kind of fun they just don't have anywhere else.

Croagh Patrick

/krohk pat-rik/

place name. sacred mountain

A much-loved place of pilgrimage in County Mayo. Unless you've climbed it barefoot, you haven't climbed it.

Croker

/krohk-ur/

place name. official GAA headquarters

Home of the all-Ireland finals and the country's most powerful residents' committee. Just ask Garth Brooks.

Cuchulainn

/koo-kul-in/

person. mythical hero

A fabled hurler noted for his big dog, his strength and his bravery. With a rollercoaster in Emerald Park named in his honour, you too can now ride the legendary warrior.

culchie

/kul-chee/

person. definitely not a Dub

Depending on who you ask, a culchie is either someone from rural Ireland, or anyone who lives outside of Dublin. A stereotypical culchie would be all too fond of red diesel, sheep, wellies, digging holes, spuds with everything, and an annual dinner dance.

cúpla focail

/koo-pla fukl/

Irish-language phrase. sporadic use of the mother tongue

You may have spent the guts of twelve years mastering the intricacies of the Irish language. Perhaps you even had a handle on the dreaded Modh Coinníollach. But school is behind you and with it your knowledge of urú's and séimhiú's. When the notion takes you, you like to throw out cúpla focail: an auld 'go raibh maith agat' here or a 'slán' there often goes down well, buíochas le Dia.

cures

/kyoorz/

noun pl. gifts for healing

You'll have heard the whispers: there's a man in Dingle who can cure shingles, a woman in Portumna who can rid you of your warts. All over the country are healers with quite specific cures for ailments like ringworm, burns, sprains or asthma. Sounds mad? Maybe. But don't knock it till you've tried it.

D

Daddy

/da-deh/

person. man of the house

Quite often a man of few words, but no can beat the Irish Daddy when it comes to kicking car tyres, hanging pictures and slipping you a few quid when you're broke.

death notices

/deth noh-tis-ez/

noun pl. breaking news

The Irish have a healthy preoccupation with death, and the death notices can often be the highest-rated segment on local radio. Many's the phone call with the parents will feature the question 'Did you hear who died?' followed by a particularly unfun version of Guess Who?

Debs

/debz/

event. end-of-school knees-up

The Debs: one of the most longed-for nights of a student's life. Who are you bringing? What are you wearing? Spray tan and an upstyle? Renting or buying a suit? The preparations are endless. Cut to the night and you get so drunk you fall alseep in your dinner, your best mate gets off with your date, you spill purple Kopparberg all down your front, and to top it all off you have to be up first thing in the morning to register for college. #BestNightEver

December 8th

/kris-mus shop-ing dey/

event. feast of the Immaculate Conception

Also referred to as 'Culchie Day', where country folk had a bit of a pray and then headed to Dublin to shop till they dropped. Traditionally a holy day of obligation, with schools closed all over the country, everyone and anyone descended on the Ilac Centre to do their Christmas shopping. Town was mobbed. Dubliners stayed at home. It took them a while, but retailers cottoned on to the fact that there was money to be made outside of Dublin and put a shopping centre or two on the outskirts of every Irish town. Now we can all shop local.

Dermot Bannon

/der-mut ban-un/

person. celebrity draughtsman

Everyone's favourite architect. Sure why would you move house when you could just get Dermot Bannon in?

dinner

/din-ur/

noun. Mammy's most important meal of the day

Dinner in Ireland is literally a moveable feast. If you're down the country, or working in farming or construction, 'dinner' is at lunchtime (and often in the oven before you're even up for breakfast). For city slickers, it's served in the evenings – except for on Sundays and at Christmas. If that's not confusing enough, 'tea' can mean a cup of tea, afternoon tea, or a light dinner. And don't even get us started on 'supper'.

directions

/di-rek-shunz/

noun pl. helpful travel hints

Ask someone for directions in Ireland and prepare to be inundated with references to pubs and churches – they're the handiest landmarks going. Even if the person you've waved down hasn't a clue where you're talking about, they'll do their best to get you some of the way. And be warned: if you get a chatty local, their directions can include a fair amount of their life story and a serving of juicy gossip.

dirty destinations

/dur-tee des-tin-ey-shunz/

noun pl. rude geography

Nobber, Blue Ball, Fannystown, Muff, Ballsbridge, Pullingtown, Letterfinish, Effin, Dicksboro, Termonfeckin, Horetown, Fartrim, Hackballs Cross, Lousybush, Balix Lower, Doodys Bottoms, Nicker, and Willyrogue Island. *snigger*

dock leaf

/dok leef/

noun. magical foliage

Nature's very own antidote to that stinger of the Irish countryside, the nettle. If you're unlucky enough to brush off one of those bad boys and instantly break out in red spots, have a scout around for a long green weed known as a dock leaf. Rub this all-powerful leaf vigorously on the bumps and hey presto, the stinging subsides. Whether this old wives' tale actually works or the pain lessens naturally as you search and rub is anyone's guess.

Donegal Postman

/dun-ee-gawl pohst-man/

person. Northern oracle

Never mind what they're doing in Met Éireann with their meteorologists and global satellite systems, the Donegal Postman holds the answer to predicting Ireland's notoriously changeable weather.

don't let the heat out!

/doh-nt let thuh heet owt/

phrase. appeal for energy conservation

The refrain bellowed by Mammies and Daddies up and down the country as soon as the doorbell rings. Either bring them in or you go out, but whatever you do 'Don't let the heat out! We're not heating the road!'

down under

/dan un-dah/

place name. strewth! Throw another shrimp on the barbie

Nearly mandatory for travelling students these days is a year down under – bunking twelve-to-a-room, working in Rosie O'Grady's pub or fruit picking from dawn till dusk. There isn't a family on the island of Ireland that hasn't had a member or two permanently relocate to the other side of the globe in search of sun, sea and Alf from *Home and Away*. What do you mean there's no such place as Summer Bay?

Dracula

/drak-yoo-la/

book. Irish vampire

Irishman Bram Stoker's masterpiece of the vampire genre went on to spawn countless imitations, tributes and adaptations, everything from *Count Duckula* to *Buffy the Vampire Slayer*. Stoker got the name 'Dracula' from a Romanian word for 'devil', but it's still a nice coincidence that 'droch ola' in Irish means 'bad blood'. Spooky.

drunk

/drunk/

adjective. after one too many

Rat-arsed, pissed, cabbaged, ossified, wasted, steaming, plastered, fluthered, gee-eyed, baloobas, jarred, in-a-heap, hammered, trolleyed, in the horrors, shit-faced, wasted, locked, sloshed, langered, blotto, full, lamped, out of your tree, scuttered, stocious, tanked, three sheets to the wind.

Dustin the Turkey

/dust-in thuh tur-kee/

person. fowl-mouthed puppet

This popular feathered Dub first featured on RTÉ's *The Den* and has been shouting 'Go on, ya good ting!' at audiences for thirty years. He has topped the Irish singles charts and won a public vote to represent Ireland at the Eurovision (with 'Irelande Douze Pointe'), campaigned in two presidential elections and became a UNICEF ambassador in 2009. Not bad for puppet poultry.

E

Eamon Dunphy

/ey-mun dun-fee/

person. grumpy critic

The 'tired and emotional', biro-throwing, ex-RTÉ sports panellist. Not a good pundit, but a great pundit.

Easter Rising

/ee-stur ry-zing/

event. springtime revolution

Ireland has always been proud of its hard-fought independence, but during the Easter Rising centenary celebrations in 2016 we went mad for it altogether. It was all Irish Volunteers this, Proclamation that and GPO the other, and the place was awash with commemorative collectibles. Anyone for an IRB baseball cap or a Patrick Pearse action figure?

Enya

/en-ya/

person. cooing millionaire

Sail Away, Sail Away, Sail Away. In 1988, the Donegal songstress took the world by storm with her debut single 'Orinoco Flow'. She went on to become the best-selling female artist in the world, with sales of over 80 million albums. She has since taken her own advice and sailed away, sailed away, sailed away from the limelight.

exaggeration

/eg-zaj-ur-ey-shun/

noun. poetic license

As the saying goes, Irish people never let the truth get in the way of a good story.

F

'Fairytale of New York'

/feyr-ee-teyl uv nyoo yawrk/

song. Ireland's Christmas anthem

A duet recorded by the Pogues and Kirsty MacColl and arguably the best Christmas song ever. The first line, 'It was Christmas Eve, babe', is enough to immediately get you in the festive spirit. And with yer man in the drunk tank singing 'The Rare Old Mountain Dew' and the NYPD lads singing 'Galway Bay', it's Irish and we're keeping it.

fake tan

/feyk tan/

noun. artificial orange-ing

Visitors to Ireland could be forgiven for thinking that its young population are descendants of Willy Wonka's Oompa Loompas. This jaundiced look is in fact purposefully acquired through the rigorous application of fake tan, taking them from milky-white maidens to bronzed goddesses. Sort of.

farmer's tan

/far-murz tan/

noun. UVB-induced skin condition

A tan everywhere but the torso. Violently red in colour. Looks great with Speedos in Lanzarote.

Father

/fah-thur/

person. man of the cloth

No, not your Daddy. The local priest.

Father Ted

/fah-thur ted/

TV prog. sitcom and national obsession

Are those cows small or far away? Go on, go on, go on, go on, go on. Down with this sort of thing! Will we ever stop talking about *Father Ted*? The sitcom first aired in 1995 and is undoubtedly the most quoted TV show in Irish history. Or is it? That would be an ecumenical matter.

Féile

/fey-la/

event. The Trip to Tipp

Before Electric Picnic there was The Trip to Tipp. During the 1990s, thousands of teenagers and twenty-somethings descended on Semple Stadium to see acts like The Stunning, Hothouse Flowers, The Cranberries and even The Prodigy. With so many unsupervised youths away from home for the first time, poor Thurles was left looking like the scene of a zombie apocalypse.

'The Fields of Athenry'

/thuh feeldz uv ath-un-ry/

song. tearjerker anthem

Written in the 1970s by Pete St. John, this ballad tells of the hardship suffered during the Great Irish Famine. The song was adopted by Irish football fans during the 1990 World Cup, and is now sung by Irish, Celtic and Liverpool fans in stadiums the world over. Most people may struggle to get through the national anthem, but we can all belt out 'The Fields of Athenry' with the best of them: 'Loooooooow liiiiiiiiiiie …'

First Communion

/furst kom-yoon-yun/

event. profitable religious ceremony

One of the biggest days in a young child's life. Preparation is key, with lessons pushed aside in favour of learning hymns and practising sticking your tongue out to receive Holy Communion. If you're lucky, you'll be picked to do a reading or sing a solo as your classmates look on in envy. And then there's the icing on the cake – the moolah, the spondulix, the cold, hard cash. Isn't that what it's all about, really? Well, that and the bouncy castle.

flat cap

/flat kap/

noun. stylish headgear

Synonymous with farmers and hipsters, the flat cap is usually made of tweed and should be worn pulled over the eyes. Best accompanied by a sheepdog or red setter.

flat 7UP

/flat sev-un up/

noun. traditional Irish home remedy

There isn't an illness in Ireland that can't be cured with a mug of flat 7UP. Simply fill a small pot, gently simmer and leave to cool slightly. Then sip away, have a nap, and you'll be right as rain.

floor fillers

/flawr fil-urz/

noun pl. guaranteed crowd-pleasers

When the mob on the dance floor starts to thin, any Irish wedding DJ worth their salt knows the old reliables to turn to. Whack on 'Come on, Eileen', 'Maniac 2000' or 'Friends in Low Places' to get things going. Get those ties on heads with 'Thunderstruck' and 'Black Betty'. And you'll never go wrong with the homegrown classics: 'Brewing Up a Storm' and 'I Useta Lover' ('the glory of her ass!').

football

/fut-bawl/

noun. not that English variety, the real thing

Gaelic is the country's obsession. And for good reason. It is the heart and soul of many communities. It brings towns together and pits counties against one another. It even has its own language: shemozzle, parallelogram, the town end, ratified!

freckles

/frek-ulz/

noun pl. skin dots

Just one of the joys of having an Irish complexion. Skin that takes on a blue tinge in winter will, once the sun comes out, either turn an attractive shade of pink or, if those Irish genes are good and strong, develop a lovely smattering of freckles. And if you're lucky that smattering may spread and join up to form one giant freckle. Nice!

fry-up

/fry-up/

noun. traditional Irish breakfast

See: breakfast roll. Take away the roll, add soda bread, a large pot of tea and a newspaper. You can't bate it.

funeral sandwiches

/fyoon-er-ul sand-wij-ez/

noun pl. bereavement sustenance

An essential part of the Irish wake. An exquisite triangular-shaped sandwich filled with a mix reserved solely for Special Occasions. Chopped tomato, lettuce, ham and mayonnaise, sandwiched between slices of fresh white bread, cut in four and loaded up on the good china plates for the mourners. Just add a cup of tea and a 'sorryforyourloss'.

Fungie the dolphin

/fun-gee thuh dol-fin/

proper noun. fisherman's friend

This famed bottlenose dolphin made his home off the coast of Dingle in the early 1980s, and a thriving boat-tour industry grew around his frequent appearances in the harbour. For years, rumours circulated that Fungie was, in fact, a number of different dolphins or even an animatron – but alas, he was spotted for the last time in 2020.

G

Gaelic Athletic Association

/gaaaaa/

proper noun. unique sports body

The organisation responsible for Ireland's native games: Gaelic football, hurling, camogie, handball and rounders. Impossible to imagine life without it – it's as Irish as St. Patrick, Peig Sayers and potatoes all rolled into one.

Gaeltacht

/geyl-tokt/

proper noun. rite of passage

Banishment to a rural village somewhere in the West of Ireland for three weeks, where you must speak Irish or you'll be sent packing. Instead of Mammy and Daddy, you have a crotchety Bean an Tí, and instead of the Friday night disco with DJ Deco, there's a céilí with Fr. Murphy. Welcome to the Gaeltacht! Sounds like hell, but the Connemara air is thick with hormones and everyone's getting the shift. What more could a teenager ask for from a summer holiday?

The Galway Races

/thuh gawl-wey rey-sez/

event. festival of horse racing and debauchery

Held every summer, half the country makes the trek to Galway for a week-long knees-up at Ballybrit. The showy political tents may be a thing of the past, but there are still plenty of ways to splash the cash – anyone want to skip the bus from Eyre Square and go halves on a helicopter from Galway Docks instead?

Game of Thrones

/geym uv thrownz/

TV prog. soft porn global phenomenon

Filmed in some spectacularly beautiful areas of Northern Ireland, *Game of Thrones* had fans from around the globe flocking to Ulster to see locations from their favourite show, even causing traffic chaos on the Dark Hedges (aka the Kingsroad). The most illegally downloaded show in the world, *GOT* had it all: a gripping storyline, high production values, award-winning acting, and a healthy helping of gratuitous nudity. Not to be watched with Great-Aunt Joan. Awkward!

Giant's Causeway

/jy-antz cawz-wey/

place name. natural wonder

On the north coast of Ireland is a unique formation of basalt rock columns descending from the North Antrim cliffs into the ocean below. The result is so dramatic that when the site was first studied in the 17th century it was believed the Causeway was man-made. Like the Mona Lisa, it's much smaller than you imagine (but equally as enigmatic).

Glenroe

/glen-roh/

TV prog. 1980s/1990s rural soap opera

For a generation of Irish children, those iconic opening titles meant one thing: have you got your homework done? Because Monday morning was only around the corner as the nation settled down to watch Dinny and Fr. Devereux and THAT greyhound, or farmer Miley's shocking roll in the hay with his wife Biddy's cousin, Fidelma. Well, holy God!

going for one

/goh-ing fur wan/

phrase. wishful thinking

Possibly the greatest and most frequent lie told in Ireland.

going out, going out-out

/goh-ing owt, goh-ing owt-owt/

phrase. declaration of intent

'Going out' can be a few drinks with your mates or the work crowd, nothing too wild. 'Going out-out', however, takes more planning – tan application, curly blow dry, shower, shave. There will be pints, there will be shots, you may even visit the smoking area. You will be hungover. Caution: 'going out' can morph into 'going out-out' once you're 'out'.

good clothes

/gud klohz/

noun pl. fancy clobber

Believe it or not, before the Celtic Tiger children often didn't have a change of clothes for every day of the week. And there was a definite distinction between your weekday clothes and your Sunday best (also worn for birthday parties, weddings and funerals). If you wore your good clothes out playing with your friends, it'd be the wooden spoon for you.

Good Friday

/gud fry-dey/

proper noun. holy day of obligation

Now Not-So-Good Friday, as in 2018 Irish pubs opened and served alcohol on Good Friday for the first time in nearly 100 years. The world didn't end, but Holy Thursday off-licence sales plummeted.

good room

/gud room/

noun. sacred space

Growing up, every Irish house had a 'good room' – a
hallowed place full of cabinets of porcelain figures,
Waterford crystal and doyleys. If Mammy and Daddy got it
for their wedding, it was in the good room. Children were
NEVER allowed in the good room. They'd only ruin it.

grand

/grand/

adjective. catch-all description

This word is used liberally by the Irish and can mean pretty
much anything. From 'exceptionally good' to 'not good
at all', and 'really very happy' to 'not happy at all', it's yet
another Irishism that you have to gauge the tone on. Best
of luck!

grand healthy smell

/grand hel-thee smel/

phrase. the aroma of cow dung

Always to be heard when townies find themselves out for a drive in the country and the car is filled with the noxious smell of manure. Sure it's nature. It's probably doing you good.

Grand Slam

/grand slam/

proper noun. rugby clean sweep

When sitting down to watch the Six Nations, there are years when the Irish would happily take victory over England at Twickenham, and years when they hope for the Triple Crown. There are years when the Grand Slam comes into view. And then there are years when all three happen at once. Best. Feeling. Ever.

grand stretch in the evenin'

/grand strech in thuh eev-nin/

phrase. when it's bright after 5pm

Not long after the clocks go forward at the end of March, people start to notice the sun setting later and the days getting longer. Thoughts turn to hazy summer evenings and romantic sunsets. And that's when you'll hear someone say, in fond tones: 'Ah, isn't there a grand stretch in the evenin'?'

Granuaile

/grawn-yoo-weyl/

person. kick-ass pirate queen

Born in 1530, Grace 'Gráinne' O'Malley grew up to be head of the O'Malley clan, and her seafaring and plundering skills earned her the nickname the Pirate Queen of Connacht. When she was a young girl, her father refused to allow her board a ship to Spain because her long, flowing locks would catch in the ropes – so Granuaile promptly cut them off. As a young woman, she divorced her husband with the succinct 'Richard Bourke, I dismiss you'. Girl power, 16th century style. Hon the Gráinne!

Guinness

/gin-is/

proper noun. Irish stout

'Guinness is good for you', as the advertising slogan went. So good, in fact, that women were routinely given a bottle of the black stuff shortly after giving birth. And doctors gave you a pint of it when you gave them a pint of blood. Fair swap.

g'way out of that

/gwey owt uv that/

phrase. ah, stop

Depending on the tone with which it's delivered, this can mean you've told a great joke, you're being turned down for a date, or you'd better hightail it out of Mr. Fitzpatrick's garden.

H

Halloween

/hol-uh-ween/

event. pagan feast

The Americans may have hijacked it, but the roots of Halloween lie in Celtic Ireland. Our ancestors believed this was the time of year when spirits moved between this world and the afterlife, and grotesque masks and costumes were used to ward them off. Not sure homemade bin bag costumes or 'sexy nurse' outfits would quite do the job.

hand-me-downs

/hand-mee-downz/

noun pl. gifts from your elders

The sheer thrill of the black plastic bag of clothes arriving from your cousins.

Hand of Henry

/hand uv on-ree/

event. international incident

The blatant handball by French striker Thierry Henry
during the second leg of the qualifiers that robbed Ireland
of our rightful place in the 2010 World Cup. Forgive him?
We'll never forgive him. Still raging, we are.

hang sangwich

/hang sang-widg/

noun. Irish delicacy

Best accompanied by a flask of steaming-hot tea, the
humble hang sangwich has provided sustenance to GAA
supporters up and down the country for years. Kept fresh
in tinfoil or the wrapper of the breadpan, this unassuming
feast is unveiled at half-time and devoured in four bites.
Delicious!

Ha'penny Bridge

/hey-pun-ee brij/

place name. Northside-Southside divide

When the Ha'penny Bridge opened in 1816, pedestrians had to pay a ha'penny to get to the other side, and it was only more than a century later that the turnstiles were lifted and pedestrians could pass freely from one side of the bridge to the other. In its wisdom, Dublin City Council has decided not to rename the bridge to account for inflation.

Healy-Raes

/hee-lee reyz/

person pl. Kerry political dynasty

The late Jackie and his sons Michael and Danny, all Kerry TDs, would be known for going to great lengths for their loyal constituents. Between them, they have also demanded the army be mobilised to tackle aggressive rhododendrons, and blamed fairy forts for causing a dip in the road, nuclear testing for the hole in the ozone layer and God for global warming. You couldn't make it up.

holy water

/hoh-lee waw-tur/

noun. hallowed H_2O

No-one should underestimate the power of dousing yourself in holy water before an exam, driving test or interview. And the further the water has travelled the better: Knock water is grand, but water from Lourdes is great stuff altogether.

Home to Vote

/hohm too voht/

proper noun. hashtag political movement

Fair play to anyone who managed to hold back the tears when #HomeToVote began trending on 21st May 2015, the day thousands of Irish ex-pats tweeted their journeys home for the marriage equality referendum. And three years later, #HomeToVote trended once again as the Irish returned home in droves to vote on the Eighth Amendment.

honorary Irish

/on-ur-ur-ee ay-rish/

person pl. adopted sons and daughters

Any celeb or dignitary who has picked up a hurley
for a photo op, including Barack Obama, Joe Biden,
Commander Chris Hadfield, and Prince Harry and Meghan.
Welcome to the family, lads.

hot-hot

/hot-hot/

adjective. we're melting here!

Eager for a break from our damp and temperate climate,
when those few days of Irish summer arrive – off come
the layers and out come the paddling pools, quicker than
you can say 'water shortage'. We love nothing more than
basking in temperatures in the early 20s. Perfect.
25 degrees? It's awful hard to work in it, but I like the
heat. 29 degrees? Ah, I like it hot, but not *hot-hot*.

hurling

/hur-ling/

noun. mash-up of hockey/rugby/UFC

The fastest field sport in the world, and not one for the faint-hearted – in the cut and thrust of the game, players are renowned for taking no prisoners. Still an amateur sport, you can see a lad break a hurley over another's head on the Sunday, and on Monday have an appointment with him for mortgage advice at your local bank.

ice-cream

/ays-kreem/

noun. dairy deliciousness

Despite living in a country where the temperature rarely exceeds 20ºC, the Irish consume more ice-cream per capita than any of our Mediterranean counterparts. Check any Irish freezer and you'll find a block of HB Raspberry Ripple lodged between the leftover shepherd's pie and a Goodfella's pizza. Now, where are those wafers?

ice-pops

/ays-popz/

noun pl. frozen E numbers

An entire generation of Irish children were practically reared on ice-pops. There was nothing more refreshing after a hard day playing Kerbs than a Captain Quencher, a Polly Pineapple, a Chilly Willy or, if your Mammy was feeling extravagant, a Fat Frog.

immersion

/ih-mur-zhuh-n/

noun. mysterious electrical device

Back before solar panels and underfloor heating, there was the immersion heater – source of all hot water for the house. Legend had it that it was more expensive to run than the International Space Station. Woe betide anyone who forgot to turn it off before they left the house.

Ireland's Own

/ar-lundz own/

magazine. homegrown reading

Visiting your Granny in hospital? Don't forget the grapes, the Lucozade and a copy of *Ireland's Own*, Ireland's longest-running family magazine. And you know you'll have a sneaky read yourself.

Irish dancing

/ay-rish dans-ing/

verb. jigging and reeling

Even without formal training, there can't be anyone in
Ireland who hasn't done 'The Walls of Limerick' at a
wedding at least once. Meanwhile, those who spent years
working hard on their 'Hop, 2, 3, 4, 5, 6, 7' and impatiently
awaiting Feis season may still have the Irish dancer calves
to prove it. Nowadays, there's definitely a lot more
hairspray, wigs, tiaras and sequins involved. And don't
forget the sock glue – the roll-on body adhesive that'll
keep those knee-highs from falling down!

Irish goodbye

/ay-rish gud-by/

noun. surreptitious exit

People are split down the middle on whether an Irish
goodbye – the act of slipping quietly out of a party – is
monumentally rude or incredibly considerate. On the
one hand, it means you haven't given people time to say
their teary farewells; on the other, you haven't ruined the
atmosphere with, well, all those teary farewells.

Irish pub

/ay-rish pub/

noun. home away from home

No matter where you go in the world, from Tokyo to Timbuktu, you'll find an Irish pub. In fact many an Irish tourist will hunt one down and spend their holiday eating stew for dinner in 30-degree heat and watching the GAA. Then there are those who just nip in to catch the 'second half' and emerge days later, jersey inside out and not a peseta to their name. Great craic altogether.

Irish summer

/ay-rish sum-ur/

event. unpredictable occurrence

Blink and you'll miss it. Normally lasts about three days and can occur anytime between April and September. When it does appear, drop everything and embrace it. Where's that factor 50?

Irish time

/ay-rish tym/

noun. casual attitude to timekeeping

For many, always being on time is something to aspire
to. But not the Irish. When a party's starting at 8pm here,
that just means anytime before midnight. For a nation
obsessed with meeting under clocks, we ain't all that good at
timekeeping.

Italia '90

/i-tal-ya nyn-tee/

event. putting 'em under pressure

From drawing against England to beating Romania in
penalties, World Cup 1990 was a tournament like no other,
with the nation's Green Army united in their love for Jack
Charlton. Did it matter that just six of the team were actually
born in the Republic? Not at all. We claimed the likes of Ray
Houghton, John Aldridge, Andy Townsend, Tony Cascarino
and Captain Fantastic Mick McCarthy as our own. We
put 'em under pressure, we put the ball in the back of the
English net, the nation held its breath, we celebrated and
then celebrated some more, then cursed Schillaci. Good
goal, though.

I will, yeah

/ay wil, yeh/

phrase. declaration of dissent

I will not.

J

jackeen

/jak-een/

person. capital dweller

A not-altogether-complimentary name for a Dubliner. A typical jackeen would be all too fond of coddle, Hill 16, pints, the M50, five of anything for a euro, and holidays down the country.

jay-walking

/jey-wawk-ing/

verb. weaving in and out between traffic

The Irish have perfected the art of walking out in front of cars without getting knocked down. Sure why would you walk down to the traffic lights when you can just plough right ahead?

jersey

/jur-zee/

noun. county t-shirt

The holiday wardrobe item of choice for Irish males abroad. A GAA jersey looks great with shorts by day and a pair of jeans at night. So versatile!

Jesus, Mary and Joseph

/jee-zus, meyr-ee und jo-suf/

phrase. invoking the holy family

Calling out to the members of the Holy Family, 'JMJ' can be used as a shocked reaction to bad news or to express gratitude after good news. Yet another slightly inappropriate Irish catch-all phrase.

Johnny Logan

/jon-ee loh-gan/

person. Eurovision legend and heartthrob

The most successful Eurovisioner of all time, Johnny 'Hold Me Now' Logan has twice sung his way to victory, as well as writing Linda Martin's winning entry, 'Why Me?'. With his smouldering good looks and soulful crooning, and that white suit, Johnny set hearts a-flutter up and down the country. *swoon*

J1

/jey wan/

proper noun. lost summer

The Irish tradition of spending a summer in the U.S. waiting on tables and ramping up the accent to get a few more tips. You might even change your name to Sinead, dye your hair red and talk about your pet leprechaun. A college education doesn't come cheap, you know!

just up the road

/just up thuh rohd/

phrase. misleading statement

Not just up the road at all, but at least several miles away.

K

Katie Taylor

/key-tee tey-lur/

person. boxer supreme

A trailblazing female boxer. Five consecutive golds at the World Championships and six at the Europeans. Olympic gold. World champion with two belts. And she's Irish, thank God.

Keano!

/kee-no/

person. Roy Keane / Robbie Keane

A handily transferable chant for Irish football fans that applied to both the irascible Corkman and the cartwheel-turning Dub. New up-and-coming football-playing Keane wanted.

Kerbs

/kerbz/

proper noun. competitive ball play

Popular ball game played across roads up and down the country. Bounce the ball off the opposite kerb to earn points, and keep scoring until you lose control of the ball. Kudos to the showboater who went for the backwards, over-the-head throw for maximum points and actually hit the kerb. What a legend.

kissing the Blarney Stone

/kis-ing thuh blar-nee stohn/

verb. perilous smooching

The ritual of leaning upside down over a parapet at the top of a castle to touch your lips to the Blarney Stone, so earning the Gift of the Gab. Considerably safer since the fitting of guide rails and cross bars in 2000, but still not one for the faint-hearted. Don't anyone tip off the Health and Safety Authority.

Knock

/nok/

place name. national shrine

A small town in Mayo where the Blessed Virgin appeared to a group of parishioners, this popular pilgrimage site now boasts a basilica and an airport. It's like Lourdes or Fátima, but with rain.

L

langer

/lang-ur/

noun. body part

Originating in the People's Republic of Cork, the term refers to the male appendage but, like 'gobshite', it may also be a term of endearment.

last orders

/last or-durz/

phrase. throwing down the gauntlet

Usually denoted by a dimming of the lights, last orders is a challenge to get as many drinks in as you can before the bar staff kick you out.

The Late Late Toy Show

/thuh leyt leyt toi shoh/

TV prog. it's beginning to look a lot like . . .

A Christmas-jumper-clad host, the latest toys and gadgets reviewed by adorably precocious kids, heart-warming musical performances and tear-jerker moments. An institution.

Leaving Cert

/lee-ving sert/

event. D-day

The national exam that decides what you're going to do FOR THE REST OF YOUR LIFE. Everything depends on it. Everything!

lighting candles

/ly-ting kan-dulz/

verb. your last resort

There is no test, trial or crisis that cannot be helped by the lighting of a holy candle. And the more candles lit for you, the better. Many churches will put local fire brigades on high alert in June each year in the run-up to the Junior and Leaving Cert exams.

line dancing

/lyn dan-sing/

verb. rhythmic cowboy stepping

A national obsession in 1990s Ireland. Community halls and hotel function rooms were packed to the rafters with men and women hitting their heels and cowboy-shuffling across the floor. Scary while it lasted, the moment passed and line dancing grapevined back to Middle America.

local headlines

/loh-kul hed-lynz/

noun pl. nosy neighbour fodder

'County Limerick Cemetery a "Death Trap"', 'One-Legged Man "Loses the Run of Himself"', 'Cork Council Starts Action against Itself over Car Park'. Although they often raise more questions than they answer, our local newspaper headlines offer an intriguing glimpse into just what is going on in Ireland's towns and suburbs. Before parents ring their kids in Canada or Australia, they'll give the paper a quick scan so they're first with the news of who scored the winning point for St. Brendan's, where the local Tidy Towns group went on their yearly day out, and who threw their garlic fries at Sergeant Murphy's car.

lock-in

/lok-in/

noun. the drinking continues

Last orders were ages ago, and the pub shutters are down. Everyone's keeping that little bit quieter, and the barman is taking breaks between pouring pints. You've only gone and got yourself into a lock-in and are now living outside the law. When you've had your fill of drink, take care to look both ways before stepping out into the street (in case the Gardaí are lying in wait).

long finger

/long fing-ur/

phrase. postpone indefinitely

A phrase that comes from the Irish 'méar fada'. Why do today what you can do tomorrow? Or the next day. Or the day after that. Irish-style planning.

long mass or short mass?

/long mas awr shawrt mas/

phrase. how long are we going to be here?

The question on everyone's lips as they try and make themselves comfortable on the wooden pews of the local church on Siobhán and John Joe's Big Day. Rule of thumb: if all the bride has done is talk about her nuptials for the last year, you're in for the long mass. Tip: make sure you get a good fry-up into you before you leave the house.

Lotto

/lot-oh/

proper noun. daydream believing

The Irish Lotto still has a charmingly small multi-million jackpot for those who haven't had their heads turned by the showy EuroMillions. But it could definitely be you.

M

Maeve Binchy

/meyv binch-ee/

person. world-famous scribe

Ireland's most-loved writer, she sold over 40 million books worldwide and blazed a trail for authors like Marian Keyes and Cecelia Ahern. Renowned for heart-warming stories and quietly feminist characters, she once said: 'I don't have ugly ducklings turning into swans in my stories. I have ugly ducklings turning into confident ducks.'

magic road

/maj-ik rohd/

noun. tarmacked surface with magical properties

Stop the car, take off the handbrake, and roll UP a hill. Abracadabra! Magic roads are mad optical illusions that occur all over the country, including behind Ben Bulben in Sligo, near Slievenamon in Tipperary, and between Dundalk and Carlingford in Louth.

Mammy

/mam-eh/

person. female giver of life

You could travel the whole world without finding someone as wonderful as the Irish Mammy. Starts hoovering when you're still in bed, has the roast beef on for dinner by 11am, won't let you out of the house without a coat, and spits on her tissue to wipe your face – and you're twenty-nine years old. Irreplaceable.

man who slipped on the ice

/man hoo slipt awn thee ays/

person. wintery fall guy

One lad's spectacular fall on icy paths during the Big Freeze of 2010, serendipitously filmed and broadcast by RTÉ. Must be the most-watched clip of the Six One News ever.

Marietta biscuits

/mar-ee-et-a biz-kitz/

proper noun pl. small and sweet confectionery

Take two, spread liberally with butter, and squeeze them together until the butter oozes out. A special Irish childhood treat.

Marty Morrissey

/mar-tee mawr-is-ee/

person. sports commentator

The man, the tan, the teeth, the hair, the ladies. The legend.

más é do thoil é

/mawsh ey duh hul ey/

Irish-language phrase. long-winded please

Often preceded by the words 'An bhfuil cead agam dul go dtí an leithreas?' ('May I go to the toilet?') Vital lingo for schoolkids.

messages

/mess-ij-ez/

noun pl. bought provisions

No, not the WhatsApp kind, but the shopping. Remember the days when kids were dispatched down to the local shop whenever the house ran out of milk, or bread … or cigarettes … or scratch cards? And if they were really lucky, they got to spend the change on penny sweets.

Micheál Ó Muircheartaigh

/mee-hawl oh mwur-a-hurt-ig/

person. GAA broadcasting legend

Guinness World Record holder for the longest career as a live match commentator, for six decades this man gifted us with classic quotes and poetry-peppered descriptions. For most, Ó Muircheartaigh was a national treasure synonymous with Gaelic games.

midnight mass

/mid-nyt mas/

event. nocturnal religious service

The annual Christmas Eve outing where prodigal sons and daughters join their parents in the pews for a blessing. Nowadays has been moved to 9pm to minimise the attendance of the inebriated, or at least to make sure they're not too inebriated just yet.

Miggeldy Higens

/mig-ul-dee hig-inz/

person. beloved leader

The ninth President of Ireland, fondly nicknamed after a primary school student struggled with the spelling of Michael D. Higgins. A lifelong politician and human-rights campaigner with the soul of a poet, Miggeldy is renowned for being a world-class orator, the ex-President of Galway United F.C, and BFFs with Martin Sheen. What a dude.

Moore Street

/mohr street/

place name. Dublin's oldest open-air fruit and veg market

'Anyone der now for de straaaaaaaaawbreeeeeeeez?'

'Are ye looking for wrapping paper, love?'

'Apples, five for feeeeefteeeeee!'

moving statues

/moo-ving stach-ooz/

noun pl. kinetic effigies

Ah, the summer of 1985, when people flocked in their droves to more than thirty villages countrywide in the wake of widespread sightings of moving statues of the Virgin Mary and other saintly figures. Rumour had it that by rubbing a handkerchief on one of these statues, you could bring back some of their divine power to a loved one at home. Best present ever.

N

names

/neymz/

noun pl. the brands our parents gave us

We Irish have beautiful names, but the spelling doesn't always make a lot of sense to foreigners – when 'si' is 'sh', and 'io' is 'u', and 'mh', 'dhbh' and 'bh' are all pronounced 'v'. And if non-gaeilgeoirs struggle with simple names like Niamh, Oisín and Sinéad, watch them try and get their heads around tricky little numbers like Saoirse, Ruaidhri or Caoilfhionn. How can any word need *so many vowels*?

negative equity

/neg-uh-tiv ek-wi-tee/

noun. when your outstanding mortgage is more than your house is worth

When the bottom fell out of the Irish housing market, up to a third of home-owners were plunged into negative equity. Back in the heady days of the Celtic Tiger, Irish people used to browse property websites for fun; now it's to check roughly how much negative equity we're still in.

Newgrange

/nyoo-greynj/

place name. Neolithic know-how

Older than Stonehenge and the Pyramids, Newgrange is a huge, circular passage grave found in Co. Meath. We're not sure exactly how they did it, but the Neolithic people who built the monument ensured that on the winter solstice, the light of the rising sun shines directly through the roof box above the main entry, illuminating the entire burial chamber for a whopping seventeen minutes. Of course, if they were *really clever*, they would have built Newgrange somewhere there was a better prospect of a cloud-free sky in December.

ninety-nine

/nyn-tee-nyn/

noun. scrumptious soft serve

Is there anything more Irish than sitting on a cold, wet beach in summer, eating a ninety-nine? A crispy, light wafer cone topped with soft, whipped ice-cream and a delicious chocolate flake. And we can all remember that day when the trainee shopkeeper lost control of the Mr. Whippy machine and you ended up with a towering ninety-nine that gave you a ten-minute brain freeze.

Nobel Laureates for Literature

/noh-bel law-ree-utz fur lit-ra-choor/

person pl. award-winning scribblers

We Irish are immensely proud of our literary heritage, and we won't have a word said against any of our four Nobel-winning writers: W.B. Yeats, George Bernard Shaw, Samuel Beckett and Seamus Heaney. But apart from things we were made learn for English exams, hands up who's actually read any of them?

notions

/noh-shunz/

noun pl. ideas above one's station

Often muttered under the breath and accompanied by a dramatic eye roll, 'notions' are far from where you were raised. Quinoa pancakes for brunch? An 'outdoor room' instead of a back garden? Garra rufa fish pedicures? Notions, all of them.

Oirish

/oy-rish/

adjective. over-'Irish'

We are constantly bemused by anyone playing up to those classic Irish stereotypes. Has anyone EVER said, 'Top o' da mornin' to ya, laddie'? Though what woman could possibly resist the *Far and Away* Oirish charm offensive: 'Yer a corker, Shannon. What a corker you are!'

Olé Olé Olé Olé!

/oh-ley oh-ley oh-ley oh-ley/

phrase (sung). Irish/Spanish cheer

This catchy little number became hugely popular in Ireland during the 1990 World Cup, when it featured heavily in the chorus of the official team song, 'Put 'Em Under Pressure'. It's simple, it's upbeat, and you can pick up the tune in about five seconds. Sure, we may have stolen it from the Spanish, but no-one sings it louder or prouder than the Irish.

Olympics

/uh-lim-pikz/

event. global games

Ireland hereby salutes our Olympic-medal-winners: from Pat O'Callaghan to Sonia O'Sullivan, Ronnie Delany to Annalise Murphy. And Michael Carruth, Katie Taylor and our army of boxers – for a small country, there's no denying we punch above our weight.

orange cheddar

/or-inj che-dur/

noun. dyed cheese

Walk into any Irish supermarket and you'll find orange and yellow cheddars from the same producer. And shoppers show a definite preference for the orange variety, buying twice as much of it as the yellow. But here's the thing: the orange cheddar is just yellow cheddar with added food colouring. Don't believe it? Do a blind taste test, and prepare to have your mind blown.

P

Padre Pio

/paw-drey pee-oh/

person. seriously high-up saint

Irish grannies are convinced this bearded, brown-robed saint will protect their grandchildren in transit. A sticker for the back window or a miraculous medal hanging from the rear-view mirror? Either way, you're all set for reversing.

parcels from America

/par-sulz frum uh-mer-i-kuh/

noun pl. goodies from far-flung relatives

Oh, the excitement in the house when the postman brought a box from that long-lost auntie in New Jersey! Filled with Mickey Mouse t-shirts and baseball caps, brightly coloured candy, and even crisp dollar bills, that package gave Irish kids a taste of the magical land of America. Nowadays, they just hop on the red-eye to JFK.

Peig

/peg/

person. údar

The best-known storyteller from the Blaskets, Peig Sayers'
Irish-language autobiography did much to put a whole
generation of secondary school students off their native
tongue. Turns out teenagers aren't mad about unremittingly
bleak island memoirs. Who knew?

Phoenix Park

/fee-niks park/

place name. Dublin's great wide open

The largest enclosed municipal park in any capital city in
Europe, it's also home to two of Irish children's favourite
things: the President and Dublin Zoo. And it's always a
great place to bring a pope.

pint glass

/pynt glas/

noun. glass designed to hold 568ml

Those pint glasses in the cupboard at home? They definitely
weren't stolen from the local pub. Definitely not.

plastic bag levy

/plah-stik bag lev-ee/

noun. moneybags

With the introduction in 2002 of a charge for plastic bags, Irish people made huge efforts to remember those feckin' bags-for-life from the designated drawer or car boot when they went shopping. After years of practice, we're getting better at it, and only about a third of shoppers can now be seen walking gingerly out of shops balancing various purchased items about their person.

Ploughing Championships

/plow-ing champ-yun-shipz/

event. annual agricultural knees-up

Every September hundreds of thousands of people attend the national championships to see expert ploughmen and women pit their skills against one another. Not a fan of ploughing? There's bound to be something that takes your fancy – the pig agility course, welly throwing, sheep shearing, cow milking or the tractor made of cheese. Hunter wellies and wax jackets optional.

poitín

/put-yeen/

noun. alcoholic rocket fuel

Formerly illegal moonshine distilled from potatoes, with an alcohol content of anything from 40–90%. Officially legalised in 1997, it has been granted special geographical status by the EU, similar to that for champagne, meaning that only poitín made in Ireland can carry the name. Often found at the back of presses and consumed when you've brought a few friends round after the pub and there's not a drop of wine or beer left.

potato

/puh-tey-toh/

noun. delicious and versatile root vegetable

The world often makes fun of the Irish for our love of the humble potato, but it's hard to top for versatility. Boiled, mashed, roasted, fried, baked or chipped? Colcannon, boxty, potato bread, dumplings or crisps? If loving spuds is wrong, we don't want to be right.

potholes

/pot-hohlz/

noun pl. rocky road

Potholes have long been an epidemic on Irish roads, particularly in more rural areas. Not all bad, they're a great place to bring your toddler for a little paddle, as long as you don't mind the speeding traffic. Rumour has it there is still more tar in the nation's cigarettes than on the roads.

pull like a dog

/pul lyk a dawg/

phrase. give it your all

This handy little phrase came from silver-medal rowers Gary and Paul O'Donovan at the 2016 Rio Olympics. The Skibbereen brothers won the hearts of the nation and became an overnight sensation with their laid-back interview technique. Paul summed up rowing with: 'It isn't too complex really. A to B as fast as you can go and hope for the best. Close the eyes and pull like a dog.' Irish can-do attitude at its best.

The Queen of Ireland

/thuh kween uv ar-lund/

film. aka Panti Bliss

An acclaimed documentary about drag queen Panti Bliss (Rory O'Neill), an important symbol of modern Ireland and a highly influential figure in the marriage equality campaign. Panti gave it socks with her Noble Call for equal rights and an end to homophobia. All hail the Queen of Ireland!

queuing

/kyoo-ing/

verb. waiting in an orderly fashion

Maybe it's in our genes, but queuing just doesn't suit the Irish. Our preference is to hang around in unruly gangs and then dive in for a free-for-all when the doors open. Much better.

The Quiet Man

/thuh kwy-it man/

film. classic 1952 flick

Take one feisty redhead, add one bolshy Yank with a penchant for dragging women around fields, add a sprinkle of lush Irish countryside and a dollop of fist-fight, and you've got everything you need for the quintessential Oirish film. Although John Ford's depiction of Ireland in *The Quiet Man* was far from accurate, it did wonders for Irish tourism as Americans flocked to the West to see the sites portrayed in the film. We're still milking it.

R

Ray Houghton

/rey how-tun/

person. celebrated Ireland and Liverpool footballer and commentator

Which goal do we love Ray Houghton more for: the one against the old enemy, the English, in Stuttgart in the 1988 European Championship, or the one against Italy in Giants Stadium in the 1994 World Cup? It's like trying to pick your favourite child. Either way, there's no chance that man has had to buy himself a pint here in thirty years.

Rebel County

/reb-ul kown-tee/

place name. Cork

The Real Capital, as Corkonians like to call it, has long had a history of not taking things lying down – not from the Vikings and not from the Dubs. Sure they're an awful shower of rowdy rebels.

redheads

/red-hedz/

person pl. ginger-topped people

Because being redheaded involves a genetic mutation, populations thrived in historically isolated communities like Ireland, Scotland and Scandinavia. Just 2% of the world's population has red hair, and those people also have fewer strands of hair, are more likely to be left-handers and are more sensitive to both pain and temperature. If they hail from Ireland, as well as the red hair they usually have pale skin and freckles: the holy Irish trinity.

red lemonade

/red leh-mun-eyd/

noun. ruddy carbonated beverage

Back when fizzy drinks were still called 'minerals', Sunday afternoon often saw the kids sent off to their own table in the pub with a bag of crisps and a red lemonade. This delicious drink was so difficult to find outside Ireland that the rumour spread that it was banned everywhere else. Made you feel dangerous and daring sipping your TK.

Red Rover

/red roh-vur/

proper noun. intermittently violent childhood game

'Red Rover, Red Rover, we call Paddy over!' Two teams line up, hand in hand, calling opposite team members over to break the chain, and baying for blood. Even with the odd broken bone or two (who's counting?), the best childhood memories are made of games like these.

referendum

/ref-uh-ren-dum/

noun. single-issue vote

Ireland's great for the referendums. While some of the most contentious and celebrated referendums have been those on social issues such as marriage equality, divorce and abortion, the electorate has been brought to the polls for all sorts of changes to the constitution, including the voting age and the death penalty, acceptance of the Good Friday Agreement, and joining the EU (and then many, many referendums on various EU treaties until we feckin' well got them right).

relations

/ri-ley-shunz/

person pl. aunts & uncles & cousins & third cousins twice removed

Growing up in Ireland, you do begin to wonder if it's possible for one Irish person *not* to be related to another somehow. 'Ah, you're not one of the Edenderry Lawlesses, are you? Sure wasn't Granny on Daddy's side a Lawless?' And repeat. And repeat.

rhyming slang

/ry-ming slang/

noun. classic Dublin humour

Dublin city is home to many statues that are rarely called by their real names, but by rhyming nicknames. There's the Floozie in the Jacuzzi, the Prick with the Stick, the Tart with the Cart, and the Hags with the Bags. And don't forget the Ace with the Bass, the Crank on the Bank and the Stiffy at the Liffey.

rhythm method

/ri-thum meth-ud/

noun. meticulous family planning

When your Mammy has seven brothers and sisters, and your Daddy has eleven.

Riverdance

/riv-ur-dans/

proper noun. Irish-dancing phenomenon

The interval act for the 1994 Eurovision held in the Point Depot, *Riverdance* gave the nation patriotic chills while taking the world by storm. Featuring the gracefully skilled Jean Butler and the alarmingly bouffanted super-stomper Michael Flatley, *Riverdance* went on to become one of the most successful dance productions in the world.

road frontage

/rohd frun-tij/

noun. marriage eligibility

Any land you own that has access to a main road – prime real estate, ready for building. Want to suss out if someone grew up in the country or the city? Throw 'road frontage' into the conversation and see if their eyes light up.

The Rose of Tralee

/thuh rohz uv tra-lee/

event. time-honoured Kerry pageant

The long-running and hugely popular annual festival where educated and accomplished women of Irish descent wear pretty dresses and sashes and titter over questions from the cheeky host about their boyfriends. And aren't they all lovely girls?

rounds

/rowndz/

noun pl. turn-taking in the purchase of alcohol

In Ireland, when someone offers to buy you a drink, there is an implicit understanding that you will return the favour. And now you're in a round, the major problems being: you're obliged to stay in the rounds system until you've bought your round, and everyone in the round has to increase their drinking speed to match that of the fastest drinker. 'Tis madness, like.

RTÉ Guide

/ar-tee-ee gyd/

magazine. TV listings

In the days before content-on-demand TV, an almost nationwide activity in December was sitting down with the Christmas edition of the *RTÉ Guide* and a red pen to mark all the films you wanted to watch and/or record. And God forbid *The Great Escape* would clash with *Willy Wonka & the Chocolate Factory*.

Ryanair

/ry-un-eyr/

proper noun. thrifty travel

From a small airline founded in 1984, Ryanair has grown to become Europe's largest carrier. Making air travel more affordable through its infamous 'no frills' approach, it often opts for less-used airports that are considerable distances from the hoped-for destination. Sure, Frankfurt-Hahn is only 126km up the road from Frankfurt. What d'ya expect for €29.99?

S

's'

/ess/

letter. unnecessary consonant

We Irish love to pluralise things that don't need pluralising. From Supervalus to Easons, and Tescoes to BTs, from Liddles to Aldis and even euros, Legos and Taytos, there is nothing we won't throw an S on the end of.

Safe Cross Code

/seyf kros kohd/

song. children's road-safety ditty

Drilled into generations of Irish children, this handy little number reminded us all how to cross the road safely. From looking for a safe place to looking all around and listening. And absolutely no leaving the kerb before you've let all the traffic pass you. 'Know the Safe Cross Code – KNOW THE CODE!'

Saipan

/sy-pan/

place name. THAT Japanese island

The somewhat unlikely scene of the greatest rift in Irish soccer, between manager Mick McCarthy and star player Roy Keane, during the 2002 World Cup. Voices were raised, things were said, lines were drawn. Even after all these years, the Team Roy or Team Mick question still divides families and friends all over the country.

salad

/sa-lud/

noun. cold comfort

On a warm summer evening, forget your couscous and fennel with pomegranate dressing – there's nothing better than an Irish salad. A hard-boiled egg, two slices of cooked ham (rolled up, for sophistication), half a tomato and a dollop of coleslaw or potato salad. If you're feeling adventurous, add a couple of slices of beetroot (from a jar, none of that fresh stuff) and salad cream to taste. And don't forget the single scallion, draped artistically across the plate, for a little *je ne sais quoi*. Haute cuisine à la Mammy.

The Shift

/thuh shift/

noun/verb. pucker up

Meet, feek, score, wear the face off, 'with', get with, get off with, get away with, mug, lob the gob, throw lips, throw the head, make out, play tonsil tennis, suck face, smooch, snog, pull, jag, maul, póg. Who said romance is dead?

shite

/shyt/

expletive. excrement

Technically a variant of 'shit', shite is used by the Irish with great fluency in a range of situations. It has myriad meanings, from noun to verb, adjective to adverb, but suffice to say that none of them reflect well on the person, thing or state of affairs to which it is applied.

sing-song

/sing-sawng/

noun. informal musical get-together

There's nothing the Irish like better than a good old sing-song, at the beginning or the end of a night. Expect to hear lots of homegrown fare like 'Raglan Road', 'Whiskey in the Jar', 'The Irish Rover' and 'The Fields of Athenry', as well as adopted favourites like 'American Pie', 'The Boxer' and 'Take Me Home, Country Roads'. Works infinitely better if there's even one person who knows enough of the lyrics to keep the others on track.

sláinte!

/slawn-cha/

salutation. traditional Irish toast

Thought to be the most-used Irish expression in the U.S., 'Sláinte!' means 'Good health to you!' as you clink glasses. Depending who you're drinking with, it can be an expression of good wishes or a statement of intent. Watch yourself.

Slane

/sleyn/

place name. scene of legendary concerts

First used for a Thin Lizzy gig in 1981, the grounds of Slane Castle in Co. Meath have played host to some of the biggest musical acts in the world including Bob Dylan, the Stones, Queen, U2, Bruce Springsteen, David Bowie, Madonna and Guns N' Roses. With up to 80,000 people going to these gigs in a small and relatively inaccessible village, attendees often have hazy memories of the looooooooooong midnight walk back to public transport.

slow set

/sloh set/

noun. erection section

When the DJ slowed it down, taking a break from the dance tunes to spin a few love songs. For the romantics, a welcome opportunity for some quality time in the arms of the object of your affection; for the rest of us, coupled shuffling around the dance floor while making awkward small talk and avoiding eye contact.

smoking ban

/smohk-ing ban/

noun. nicotine no-no

In 2004, Ireland became – rather unexpectedly for anyone who'd ever lived or socialised here – the first country in the world to outlaw smoking in all enclosed workplaces. Since then, there's mighty craic to be had outside pubs with the huddled smoking masses, and the Irish have become world-champion smirters (combined smokers + flirters).

smuggling sausages

/smug-ul-ing saw-sij-ez/

verb. criminal act involving meat

This is simultaneously not as filthy and just as filthy as it sounds. The Irish fry-up and Irish tea are the top two things that we miss when we go abroad, and many Irish mammies have been caught sneaking through customs with large amounts of vacuum-packed sausages secreted in their luggage, destined for their emigrant sons and daughters.

soft day

/sawft dey/

phrase. misty precipitation

When it's not quite raining and it's not quite dry, and droplets of rain seem to hover in mid-air, then 'it's a soft day, thank God'. Like the Inuits have fifty words for snow, the Irish have a whole range of phrases for describing a rainy day.

sorry, sorry

/saw-ree saw-ree/

phrase. repeated expression of regret

We Irish may be shameless in our use of colourful language, but in everything else we're cripplingly apologetic. Especially when we've done nothing wrong. Like when *they* clearly banged into us. When *they're* blocking our path. When *they've* forgotten something from our order or left us short-changed. And if we have to send back inedible food in a restaurant? There just aren't enough sorries in the world. (Much better to say nothing at all and spend the entire drive home complaining about how overdone the cod was.)

spice bag

/spys baag/

noun. delicacy from Irish Chinese takeaways

Created in Ireland and inspired by Asian cuisine (but tenuously so), the hugely popular spice bag comprises breaded or battered chicken, chips, sliced peppers and onions, and a mystery blend of spices. It tastes a lot like the smell that wafts from the external wall vents of your local Chinese takeaway. Recently spotted on the menu of a burger joint in Washington, D.C., of all places, the spice bag is so delicious we couldn't have hoped to keep it to ourselves for long.

Spire of Dublin

/spy-ur uv dub-lin/

proper noun. mid-town monument

This pointed, stainless-steel sculpture reaches 120m into the sky from the middle of Dublin's O'Connell Street. Controversial when it was first erected in 2002, these days people walking past tend to largely ignore it, except for the various religious fundamentalists who congregate around its base, eager to share their views. Some of the Spire's imaginative nicknames include the Stiletto in the Ghetto, the Nail in the Pale and the Erection at the Intersection.

Star Wars

/star wawrz/

film. epic sci-fi

No nation was happier than ours when Kerry's breathtaking Skellig Islands were chosen as the location for scenes in the *Star Wars* movies *The Force Awakens* and *The Last Jedi.* At last, we could legitimately embrace Luke Skywalker as one of our own. We knew it.

stew

/styoo/

noun. lip-smacking meat dish

Considered by many as Ireland's national dish, Irish stew is made from slow-cooked lamb, potatoes and onions, and sometimes carrots, turnips or pearl barley, though the exact list of ingredients is open to heated debate. (There is a powerful contingent that insists it MUST be beef and not lamb.) Your own favourite recipe will likely be what you inherited from Mammy or Daddy, because no-one makes stew like you have in your own house.

St. Anthony

/seynt an-tun-ee/

person. holy man in charge of lost stuff

Lost something? Just say a quick prayer to St. Anthony and it's sure to turn up in the last place you look.

St. Brigid

/seynt brij-id/

person. Ireland's lesser-known patron saint

Born in the 5th century and raised by druids, St. Brigid is the patron saint of, among other things, beer, dairy workers, cattle, blacksmiths, chicken farmers, printing presses, sailors and Florida. But for most of us, Brigid will always be synonymous with that tricky woven cross we had to make every 1st February. The trauma.

St. Patrick

/seynt pat-rik/

person. Ireland's better-known patron saint

The inspiration for world-class parades, ironically Patrick was not actually Irish at all. He is thought to have been kidnapped from Wales by Irish pirates in the 5th century, when he was a teenager. After his escape back home, he trained as a cleric and returned to Ireland as a missionary, impelled by a holy vision. By the 7th century, he was already worshipped as Ireland's patron saint, and his reputation only grew from there. Every Irish child knows that St. Patrick used the shamrock to teach his followers about God, Jesus and the Holy Spirit, and that he single-handedly drove all of the snakes out of Ireland. Hallelujah!

St. Patrick's Day parade

/seynt pat-rikz dey puh-reyd/

event. annual walkabout

A worldwide phenomenon held each year on 17th March. The first St. Patrick's Day parade took place in New York in 1762 and went on to spawn imitations not only in known strongholds of Irish emigrants in the US, Australia and New Zealand, but also in more unexpected locations like Brazil and Argentina, India and Japan, and – fun fact – the tiny Caribbean island of Montserrat, which is the only place outside of Ireland where St. Patrick's Day is a public holiday.

Sudocrem

/soo-doh-kreem/

proper noun. Irish panacea

Originally developed to treat nappy rash, such is the magical reputation of this healing ointment that there isn't an ailment some Irish Mammy hasn't tried it on – from acne and sunburn to sprains and concussion. Call it 'Sudo-KREM' if you must, but to us it'll always be 'Sudo-CREAM'.

Supermac's

/soo-per-maks/

proper noun. Irish fast food

Chances are, if there's a Supermac's in your town, you're going to end up there after the pub. Offers the usual selection of fast food but is particularly popular for its fries – curry fries, garlic fries, cheese fries, taco fries, or any combination. You don't *truly* know someone unless you've seen what they order from Supermac's.

T

talk to Joe

/tawk too joh/

verb. very public counselling session

Neighbours playing music too loud? Waiting three years to get a specialist to take a look at your dicky hip? Hotel bed too lumpy? Whatever you do, don't complain to the Gardaí, the HSE or hotel management. Just talk to Joe Duffy. The liveline is open . . .

Tayto

/tey-toh/

proper noun. world-beating potato crisp

The snack so mighty that it even got its own theme park, Tayto was the first ever cheese and onion crisp – created by Irish man Joe Murphy in 1954. (How did the world survive without cheese and onion flavour until 1954??) Deliciously addictive, no less than 10% of the national potato crop goes into making Tayto, and more than 525 packs are sold every single minute. That is a serious lorry-load of crisp sandwiches.

tea

/tee/

noun. nectar of the gods

Consuming on average 2.2kg of tea per head each year, the Irish are the second biggest tea drinkers in the world (beaten only by the caffeine-soaked Turks). We all know exactly what colour our tea should be, too, and would be able to pick it out of a line-up – that delicate balance of just the right strength of brown tea mixed with just the right amount of pale milk. If you find someone who can get that balance and make your tea just right, marry them on the spot.

Temple Bar

/tem-pul baar/

place name. area of Dublin south of the Liffey just over the Ha'penny Bridge

A centre of culture by day and buzzing hotspot by night, this is ground zero for most Dublin stag and hen nights. And the reward for battling your way to a pub through the inappropriately costumed crowds? Steadily rising prices as the night goes on. Good job they take Visa.

thanking the bus driver

/thank-ing thuh bus dry-vur/

verb. commuter gratitude

Sit on a bus in Ireland for more than a few stops and you'll hear a chorus of thanks given to the driver as passengers alight. An Irish thing, apparently. But sure isn't it only good manners?

thanks, Penneys

/thangks, pen-eez/

phrase. compliment deflection

The entire Irish race is famous for our complete inability to take a compliment. In years gone by, when faced with a kind word about something we were wearing, we would have bowed our heads in shame. But nowadays, there's a simple little phrase we can use in response: 'Thanks, Penneys.' It's the modern Irish equivalent of 'What? This old thing?'

thatched cottage

/thach-d kot-ij/

noun. traditional dwelling

Long a romantic symbol of Ireland, with their whitewashed stone walls and straw roofs, there are now only about two thousand of these cottages left in the country. Back in the 1800s, a one-room thatched cottage could easily house not only the whole family (including seven or eight children) but also the pig and a flock of hens. Cosy!

tin whistle

/tin hwis-ul/

noun. Irish penny whistle

The tin whistle is one of the most common instruments played in traditional Irish music, and in the hands of an expert can carry the sweetest of melodies. Unfortunately, due to its apparent simplicity, it's also the number-one choice for Irish primary school music classes. The only thing worse than listening to one tone-deaf child learning to play the tin whistle? Listening to A WHOLE CLASS of children blowing tunelessly into tin whistles. Your poor ears will never be the same again.

Tír na nÓg

/teer na nohg/

place name. mythical land of perpetual youth

In this favourite Irish myth, strapping stud Oisín is lured by the otherworldly Niamh to join her in Tír na nÓg, the land of eternal youth. When he returns to Ireland – despite Niamh's warnings – as soon as he touches the ground he ages instantly and dies soon after. One of the many feel-good Irish legends. Just ask the Children of Lir.

Titanic

/ty-tan-ik/

proper noun. ill-fated ocean liner

The 'unsinkable' *Titanic* was built in the Belfast shipyards and had its last port of call at Cobh, Co. Cork, before tragedy struck halfway across the Atlantic. The ship and its story have long captured the imagination of the Irish and spawned the hugely successful *Titanic* movie starring Leonardo DiCaprio and Kate Winslet (whose heart went on and on and on).

Tom Crean

/tom kreen/

person. unsung hero

At a time when it was difficult enough to get from one end of Ireland to the other, an intrepid Kerryman left the green, green grass of home and headed for the Antarctic. A member of Captain Scott's ill-fated quest to the South Pole, Crean actually took part in more polar expeditions than any other explorer of his generation. He eventually returned to his beloved Annascaul, opened a pub and swapped pulling sledges for pulling pints. Some man for one man.

townie

/tow-nee/

person. country town dweller

Live in a small town in Ireland? To a Dub, you're a culchie. To a culchie, you're a townie.

tribunals

/try-byoon-ulz/

noun pl. long-running public inquiries

Since the not-as-tasty-as-it-sounds Beef Tribunal in the
1990s, it seems like Ireland is always holding a tribunal –
and it's probably been going on about twice as long as it
was supposed to, costing the taxpayer millions extra into
the bargain. Top of the heap there is the Mahon Tribunal
on corruption in planning, which started life as the Flood
Tribunal and lasted from 1997 to 2013. Another couple of
years and it could have legally had its first drink.

Trócaire box

/throw-kra boks/

proper noun. cardboard charity

For years, the Trócaire box has been a fixture of Lent in
most Irish households, earning millions for overseas aid
work. A little cardboard receptacle for collecting loose
change throughout those six holy weeks, many families
had enforced payment for 'breaking Lent'. For the less
scrupulous, it was always a good source of change for the
bus – just don't forget to top it up again before handing
it over.

The Troika

/thuh troy-ka/

proper noun. friends with benefits?

A bunch of stylish Europeans who rode into town and gave us a bit of a dig-out when times were tough. Danke schoen, bankers!

Twelve Pubs of Christmas

/twelv pubz uv kris-mus/

event. modern Yuletide tradition

Thought to have originated in Dublin, the Twelve Pubs of Christmas has taken Ireland by storm. Each year, the month of December sees hordes of Christmas jumper-clad revellers descend upon twelve pubs in succession, partaking of a drink in each one. This is serious endurance drinking, not to be attempted by anyone with a fondness for their liver.

U

Uachtaráin na hÉireann

/ook-tar-awn na heyr-in/

person pl. elected heads of state

Since the adoption of our new constitution in 1938, Ireland has had nine presidents, from Irish-language activist Douglas Hyde to fire-in-his-belly speaker and all-round national treasure Michael D. Higgins. The election of humanitarian Mary Robinson in 1990 – the first woman to hold the office – made everyone sit up and take notice. We voted in another woman and the first Northern Irelander, Mary McAleese, straight after. While no-one's entirely clear on what the president can and can't do legally, that doesn't stop us from being fiercely proud of them.

uilleann pipes

/ill-un pypz/

noun pl. Irish bagpipes

Named for the Irish word for 'elbow', the uilleann pipes rest on the piper's knee while both hands play and one of the elbows pumps air in. Notoriously difficult to master, it is said that it takes seven years' practice followed by seven years' playing to make a piper. Now that's commitment.

U.K.

/yoo key/

place name. United Kingdom

There's no denying that we have a long and complicated relationship with our neighbours across the water. Nowadays, a sure-fire way to irk an Irish person is to call Ireland part of the U.K. The ensuing (quite tetchy) discussion may involve mention of Great Britain, Northern Ireland, the British Isles, the Republic of Ireland and the island of Ireland, and possibly even the drawing of complex Venn diagrams.

unnecessary journeys

/un-nes-uh-ser-ee jur-neez/

phrase. risky trips to lark about in bad weather

'Don't make unnecessary journeys. Don't take risks on treacherous roads.' RTÉ reporter Teresa Mannion spawned a viral dance hit with her heartfelt pleas during Storm Desmond in December 2015.

USA biscuits

/yoo-es-ey biz-kitz/

proper noun pl. 100-year-old confectionery

Sounds crazy, but it's true: the USA tin of biscuits was named when America joined World War I and everyone was just mad for the Yanks. For many years this has been the ultimate Christmas tin of biscuits, a favourite in Irish households with its various chocolate-covered shapes and the much-sought-after jammy dodgers, pink wafers and bourbons. Just don't start the second layer before the first is completely empty, or there'll be ructions.

U2

/yoo too/

proper noun. middle-aged Irish rockers

Founded in 1976 and initially called Feedback, then The Hype, U2 have released fifteen studio albums and are renowned for massive stadium tours. U2 is also a handy language to talk with foreigners – there's hardly a human on the planet who hasn't heard of them.

V

Van the Man

/van thuh man/

person. bluesy moondancer

The Northern Irish singer-songwriter and instrumentalist Van Morrison, whose soulful voice makes brown-eyed girls up and down the country run for the dance floor shouting 'This is my song, this is my song!' as soon as they hear the first bar of the much-loved classic. Tune.

Vikings

/vy-kingz/

person pl. ancient and hirsute Scandinavian pirates

Back in the early 9th century, fleets of Viking raiders arrived on Irish shores in longships. Initially violently plundering their way around the island, they eventually settled and intermarried, becoming permanent fixtures here. But apart from some of the most common Irish surnames, the first Irish coins, the development of the cities of Dublin, Waterford, Cork and Limerick, the creation of trade routes with Europe, and the building of Christ Church cathedral, what have the Vikings ever done for us?

visitors

/viz-i-turz/

person pl. posh guests

'We're having VISITORS.' There was always a flurry of
activity in the house before visitors arrived, whether it
was Great-Aunt Nora, the well-to-do neighbour or the
parish priest. Visitors' tea was served in a cup and saucer,
with dainty slices of leftover Christmas cake and triangular
sandwiches – a rectangular cut would have brought shame
on the house.

W

wake

/weyk/

noun. final vigil

A great Irish tradition of keeping a dearly departed loved one company before the funeral. Particularly in rural areas, huge numbers of friends and family will visit the open coffin in the family home to pay their respects. As the night goes on, solemn sadness can often turn into raucous celebration of the person's life. Now that was a GREAT wake.

wallpapered schoolbooks

/wawl-pey-perd skool-bukz/

noun pl. bulletproof books

Back in the day, before parents' wallets could stretch to sticky-backed contact paper, most Irish kids had their books covered in leftover scraps of the sitting-room wallpaper. Nothing says 'I'm serious about homework' like magnolia woodchip.

Wanderly Wagon

/wan-der-lee wag-un/

TV prog. classic children's series

Airing on RTÉ from 1967 to 1982, this was a much-loved TV show about a flying covered wagon and a motley crew of human and puppet characters including O'Brien and Godmother, Judge the dog, the bearded sweetshop owner Fortycoats (who even got his own spin-off), and arch-villain Sneaky Snake, voiced by Frank Kelly. Mention it to Irish forty- and fifty-somethings and watch them get all teary-eyed with nostalgia.

way with words

/wey with wordz/

phrase. Irish slang

Bang on, cat, gas, holy show, up to 90, bad dose, banjaxed, brutal, savage, scarlet, whisht, mot, oul fella, gaff, sca, donkey's years, leg it, take it handy, act the maggot … When it comes to crazy slang, you'll never beat the Irish.

weather envy

/weth-ur en-vee/

noun. post-holiday blues

The last thing an Irish person wants to hear on arrival back from an expensive foreign holiday is that the weather at home was only MEDITERRANEAN while they were away. Gutted.

weddings

/wed-ingz/

noun pl. nuptial shenanigans

The Irish wedding is great craic altogether. From the sneaky pint for the groom before the ceremony, to the bride's tardy arrival, to half the guests slyly keeping an eye on the match in the hotel bar, to the father-of-the-bride's weepy speech at dessert. And once the four-course meal is over at 9pm, there's just time for an hour or two of dancing before the poor, famished guests are served up mountains of cocktail sausages, Tayto sandwiches and wedding cake. And then there's the residents bar . . .

Wee Daniel

/wee da-nyel/

person. every Mammy's favourite

Ireland's answer to Johnny Cash, Daniel O'Donnell is renowned for hailing from Donegal, and loving his Mammy and ensuite bathrooms.

Wexford strawberries

/weks-furd straw-breez/

proper noun pl. red fruit from the sunny south east

The Model County has long been known for producing the most delicious strawberries in all of Ireland. And there's no surer sign of the arrival of summer than roadside stalls with hand-written signs selling the first Wexford strawberries of the year. Fruity-licious.

Wild Atlantic Way

/wyld at-lan-tik wey/

proper noun. west-coast wonders

This 2,500km touring route along the Atlantic coast of Ireland, officially launched in 2014, has proved hugely popular with tourists and takes in world-class beauty spots like the Cliffs of Moher, Connemara, the Skelligs, Baltimore and Doolin. Fair play to the genius who came up with this idea in a brainstorming meeting.

Winning Streak

/win-ing streek/

TV prog. lucrative quiz show

Uncover three stars on a National Lottery scratch card and you might just find yourself in the parallel universe that is *Winning Streak*. Full of contestants who look like rabbits in headlights and a self-conscious audience holding up homemade marker-and-cardboard signs, this old-school format show still pulls in the viewers on a Saturday night. And despite your cynicism, you'll be on the edge of your seat when Mary's trying to decide if she'll take the ten grand or the holiday, and Liam's all set to spin the wheel. Come on, the million!

Women's Christmas

/wi-minz kris-mus/

event. girls' night out

Also known as Little Christmas or Nollaig na mBan, Women's Christmas is celebrated on 6th January. Tradition had it that women could put their feet up while the menfolk ran around after them, but sure we're all equal now so we just get the gals together and go for a slap-up meal instead.

X

The X Factor

/thee eks fak-tur/

TV prog. glorified singing competition

The Irish talent on this long-running TV show ranged from the sublime, with Dublin diva Mary Byrne, to the ridiculous, with Jedward. And viewers loved judge Louis Walsh's catchy little phrases and unexpected expressions. But easily topping the popularity stakes was Mullingar charmer Niall Horan and his One Direction bandmates. Millions of teenage girls worldwide will forever be grateful.

x-rated

/eks-rey-tud/

adjective. nationwide blacklisting

With the Catholic Church at the helm for so long, it's no wonder the Irish censor banned so much, including books like Brendan Behan's *Borstal Boy* and Edna O'Brien's *The Country Girls*, and films like Monty Python's *The Life of Brian*. Interestingly enough, James Joyce's *Ulysses* was never banned as a book (the publisher didn't even bother trying to sell it here), but the movie version was labelled 'subversive to public morality'. Proper order.

Xtra-vision

/eks-tra-vizh-un/

proper noun. Netflix, 1990s style

The countrywide chain of video libraries was THE place to be on a Friday or Saturday night, with rows and rows of exciting New Releases just waiting to be picked up and brought to the counter. If you were lucky, you might manage to sneak a 15s movie past your parents. If you were unlucky, you'd put the video in only to find that the chancer who had it the night before never rewound it. And if you were really unlucky, you'd miss the 7.30pm return deadline. That fine would sit unpaid on your account for AGES.

XXXX

/eks-eks-eks-eks/

noun. filthy language, just filthy

God knows, the Irish have never been shy about peppering their speech with plenty of curses. We have adopted the F word as one of our own, and foreigners are often impressed by our litany of home-grown slurs – from bollix, eejit and fecker, to gobshite, hoor and wagon. It's not cursing if an Irish person says it – it's just f#@*ing talking.

Y

yoke

/yohk/

noun. thing (non-specific)

In Ireland, when someone's talking to you about a 'yoke', they're unlikely to be discussing anything egg-related. Confusingly, 'yoke' has two quite different meanings: one is a catch-all word for anything we can't think of the name of right then ('Give us that … yoke, will ya?'), and the other is a nickname for ecstasy. Depending on the company you keep, use with caution.

young people of Ireland

/yung peep-ul uv ar-lund/

phrase. papal greeting

In September 1979, the Pope Himself took a trip here to address the 'young people of Ireland', ensuring a lack of originality when it came to picking the young fella's name. If you're Irish, male and born in 1980, chances are you're named John Paul. See: contraception. See also: rhythm method.

yous

/yooz/

pronoun. second person plural

The Irish plural of 'you', as in the typical Mammy refrain, 'Where are yous going without yizzer coats on?' We're not alone on this – other people to use 'yous' are the English, Scots, Aussies, New Zealanders and South Africans, as well as those from Ontario, Philadelphia, New York and Boston. But given the high level of historical Irish emigration to everywhere on that list, it's quite possible that we were responsible for bringing it there in the first place. Yous can thank us later.

Z

Zig & Zag

/zig und zag/

person pl. popular alien puppets

The hilarious characters from RTÉ 2's long-running *The Den* who kept children entertained every weekday after school with their madcap antics and alter-egos Captain Joke, Cousin Nigel and Sunny Daze, and additional characters Zuppy, Dustin the Turkey, Soky and the evil Podge. The world's best-ever puppet alien brothers – and there's a generation of Irish who will still fight you if you claim otherwise.

'Zombie'

/zom-bee/

song. Cranberries track

A protest song penned by the Limerick band's lead singer, the late Dolores O'Riordan, that made them a worldwide sensation. The poignant lyrics and grungey bass made it the perfect soundtrack for teenage angst. Leave me alone, Mam!

Zozimus

/zoz-i-mus/

person. 19th-century street poet

Known as the 'Blind Bard of the Liberties', Michael Moran was born in Dublin's Faddle Alley in 1794 and lost his sight when he was only a few weeks old. He was famous for reciting lengthy poems (his own and others') while standing at Wood Quay or Essex Bridge in his long-caped coat and stove-pipe hat. Ah, they just don't make them like that anymore.

ABOUT THE AUTHORS

Both children of the 1980s, Kunak & Sarah spent their
childhoods practising the Safe Cross Code and drinking
red lemonade, blissfully unaware that bowl haircuts and
dungarees were not a good look. Thankfully they grew up
to become waaay cooler adults (or so their mammies tell
them). Kunak works in publishing and Sarah in education.

Also by

Kunak McGann & Sarah Cassidy

IRISH
MAMMY
in your
POCKET
Sarah Cassidy & Kunak McGann

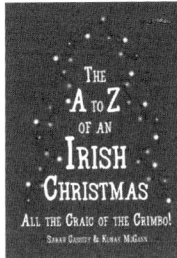
THE
A TO Z
OF AN
IRISH
CHRISTMAS
ALL THE CRAIC OF THE CRIMBO!
SARAH CASSIDY & KUNAK McGANN

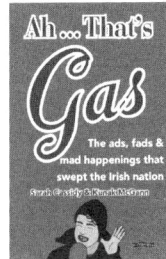
Ah ... That's
Gas
The ads, fads &
mad happenings that
swept the Irish nation
Sarah Cassidy & Kunak McGann

And by Kunak McGann

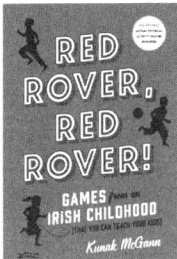
RED
ROVER,
RED
ROVER!
GAMES from an
IRISH CHILDHOOD
(THAT YOU CAN TEACH YOUR KIDS)
Kunak McGann

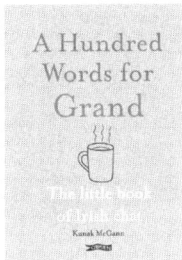
A Hundred
Words for
Grand
The little book
of Irish Chat
Kunak McGann

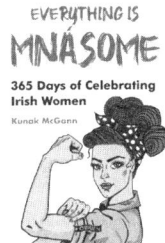
EVERYTHING IS
MNÁSOME
365 Days of Celebrating
Irish Women
Kunak McGann

Great books from

O'BRIEN

Hundreds of books
for all occasions

From beautiful gifts to books you'll want to
keep forever! The best writing, wonderful
illustration and leading design.
Discover books for readers of all ages.

Follow us for all the latest news and
information, or go to our website
to explore our full range of titles.

TheOBrienPress   TheOBrienPress

OBrienPress   TheOBrienPress

Visit, explore, buy
obrien.ie